BRUMMIE GIRLS DO SOCIAL WORK

D1799396

BRUMMIE GIRLS DO SOCIAL WORK

SHARI KING AND NICOLA BROWN

YOUCAXTON PUBLICATIONS

OXFORD & SHREWSBURY

Contents

Declaration

We would like to make it clear that the service users we have helped in the course of our work are not the people the reader will meet in this book. Names, nationalities, locations and some genders of staff and service users have been changed for complete confidentiality.

We may have used fictional names—but the emotions and incidents that are typical within our field of work are real.

Shari King & Nicola Brown

Acknowledgements

Thank you to the social-care professionals who continue to support vulnerable people, to the people who have allowed us to make a difference in their lives and to those that have supported the authors in developing into professionals who will continue on the path to further growth.

We would also like to thank our love ones who have supported us through our career paths—and we would like to thank one another.

Chapter 1

Why Social Work?

BRIEF BACKGROUND: SHARI KING

So here is where I share a brief background about me. I am twenty-eight years old born and raised in the West Midlands. I was born to two parents both separately encompassing the epitome of ambition with my mum working for a bank and my dad a psychotherapist. I was raised however in a single parent home because my parents split when I was young. I did well in school during my school years but got in trouble for talking a lot—although I maintained good grades.

My main attributes flourished in the performing arts. I sang, danced and acted right up until college and this kept me in the so called "popular groups". I gained 8 A-C GCSEs prior to going on to study sociology, psychology, drama and music in college at A level.

My first year of college was a sham. I scored U's in all my work, which was an absolute shocker. Having always maintained stable grades at school, A-levels were no joke, plus the new "your life is your own destiny" motto that college provided contributed towards my terrible grades. My second year involved a life in the library to ensure that I left college with some appropriate grades to enable me to go to university.

I applied for a place at the local university to study Social Work practice. I never wanted to become a Social Worker and I really wanted to become a psychologist. Social Work was just going to be the platform to provide me with the skills and experience that would prepare me to then practice as a psychologist.

After college I gained the grades to enable me to go to university although I deferred my place because I had the bright idea of working full time in order to earn a good salary. Once I started the life of nine-to-five however the money was no longer appealing. I spoke to my mum and told her that I thought I wanted to go to university. By this time, the course that I had deferred was due to start in three days. My mum called the university and requested that they put me on the course. Down to my mum's persuasion and things being in my favor that day, I got onto the course.

And that, funnily enough, was where I was reunited with Nicola. We had initially met in college when we were both sixteen years old. We had grown very close during the first year although we ended up drifting apart over the second year. I had no idea until I started the course that she was due to start Birmingham city University or that she had chosen to become a Social Worker.

BRIEF BACKGROUND: NICOLA BROWN

So a little about me, I'm twenty-eight years of age. Born and raised in the West Midlands. I had a relatively positive childhood with lots of positive, happy, childhood memories.

I did not settle very well in school, especially primary school. I did not want to learn, so I didn't and I learnt very little. In secondary school I was still quite naughty but managed to got my head down and catch up. I worked very hard, obtained my GCSEs and progressed to college where I gained A level's in psychology, sociology, law (AS-Level) and general studies.

Honestly, for me there was no initial pull into Social Work. There was a lot of pressure at the college I attended to progress to university. I struggled to find something to do. I wanted to go on to study law but it did not seem meaningful. It was while looking through different job descriptions that I came across Social Work. The job description requires a people person, someone with empathy, someone who is honest, open and able to challenge; I felt like I ticked all of the boxes. I decided to apply and I obtained a place at a local university starting in September 2005. I was not aware that Shari had applied too but when we started the course we were reunited. We knew each other from college and had remained friends since completing our A level's.

OUR JOURNEY AFTER UNIVERSITY: SPOKEN BY SHARI KING

The course commenced as expected. Aspects of it were valuable especially the Social Work placements. Each student was required to complete two sixty-day and one ninety-day placement. Each placement gave hands-on practice in various areas of Social care. The last placement had to be within a statutory environment, within a Social Work team. Each placement was assessed by practice and a written portfolio. In addition to this, the Social Work course consisted of modules that required a written assignment with a 40%

rate required. At the end of the course we were required to complete a dissertation, which was the most challenging part of the whole experience.

We received our grades in September 2008 and graduated in March 2009. Nicola got a 2.1 BSc (Hons) in Social Work and I came out with a 2:2 due to leaving someone's initials on the portfolio from my last placement. Back then, breeching confidentiality in your work, such as leaving a service user's name in a document, which would enable people to identify the service user and your grade would be capped at 40% but, luckily, that has now changed, with grades resulting from the level of work you provide.

Although we trained on the same courses our experience from then on led us to take different pathways in our Social Work careers.

Nicola was confident that she wanted to practice in children and families Social Work. She started practicing in May 2008 in a busy children and families Social Work team. Having practiced in various areas of children and families, she progressed from being a newly qualified Social Worker through to Senior Practitioner. Nicola now has experience in Care Management, Duty and Assessment, multi-agency referral safeguarding hubs and Child-in-Care teams. She has undertaken complex work in a range of areas including Section 47, Child Protection enquiries, Child Protection plans, child-in-need pre-proceedings, care proceedings including high court, private law, permanency, rehabilitation and looked-after children's cases.

My pathway in adults arose due to my last placement being within an adults care management team. I did not choose to start work straight away and it was a year after graduating that I decided to use my degree. I signed onto an agency and was able to start straight away due to the experience I had received in my statutory adults placement. I started in care management and have spent the last six years within every Adults Directorate from London to the West Midlands. I have worked for hospital teams, learning-disability teams, physical-disability and community mental health teams. Some of the work I have undertaken has consisted of social care assessments under the Community Care Act, mental-capacity assessments, best-interest assessments, reviews, budget requests, hospital discharges, tribunal reports and adult safeguarding. I have now progressed into becoming a lead practitioner where I manage staff which has enabled me to further gain insight into the role and challenges of Social Work.

The diverse mixture of people, classes, age and race that we have worked with has helped us to grow in the way we view the world and has also highlighted significant difficulties that so many people experience each day—which are not known unless you are going through similar situations.

Despite working in different areas of Social Work Nicola and I have always remained close even when living in different cities. Our friendship, love and our interest in the diverse areas of Social Work in which we practice inspired us to start writing together.

THE PURPOSE

Our purpose in this book is to enlighten, teach, highlight, encourage and inform people about the practice of Social Work. It is not to tell someone else's story but our own story and how we have dealt with the various situations that we have encountered. We have portrayed this career in its true light with all elements and many that are common to other jobs. There are positive, negative and humorous experiences that we also wanted to share.

Chapter 2

Scenario 1

ALWAYS BRING A BOTTLE

I remember visiting a home during the month of Eid and was welcomed in by a family whom I was visiting in order to complete an assessment on their daughter. The father asked me whether I would like a drink and I politely said "no thank you". To my surprise however, two minutes later he arrived back into the living room with a cold glass of orange juice. Now, unfortunately, I have my own obsessive-compulsive qualities and was not going to be drinking the drink which was left for me. I offered it back to the family who advised that they were fasting and could therefore not drink it either.

Let's just say, one felt rather guilty leaving the house that day.

Tips

Most people are welcoming and invite you into their home as they would any other visitor. There have been many occasions when I have been offered any array of snacks and beverages although I am not one to eat or drink from strangers. This is of course my personal issue although, as a professional, it is always crucial to maintain your role as a professional in order to prevent too much familiarity. One cup of tea can lead to too much comfort. My way of politely saying no is to bring a bottle with me when doing a home visit. Not that I'm thirsty but so that those I am visiting can see that I already have a drink to tend to my needs.

I have also found it reliable to visit after lunch or first thing in the morning because you can use the excuses: 'I've just had breakfast' or 'I've just had my lunch'. Both will be less offensive than merely saying 'no' when in someone's home.

Scenario 2

DIRTY BUM

The second case I ever dealt with. I turn up at the house. There is a young boy aged seven fixing the door handle. It must be Caiden; he's supposed to be in school and has very poor attendance. Caiden shouts to his mum "Mum the social lady's here". Mum comes to the door. Her hair is not combed and her clothes have seen better days. Her teeth are very stained and she looks quite aged. Mum is very pleasant and invites me in. The first thing I see is a brown Staffordshire bull terrier running towards me. I have white trousers on and, although I usually like dogs, this one does not look like he's stopping. He dives at me leaving muddy prints all over the tops of my legs. He's very excitable and uncontrollable like a little tiger bouncing all over the place. Mum takes hold of his collar, screams and escorts the dog into the kitchen. I'm left with very muddy white trousers. But wait—it gets worse. Let's just say, after I leave I have a nice sticky, grubby bum to match my muddy legs. Straight to Asda to buy some new trousers.

Tips
Lesson to all: do not wear your new or white clothes to do home visits. You never know what kind of situation you're going into.

Homes can be smoky, unhygienic or even cluttered. Take a spare coat, body spray and hand sanitizer.

This is not about passing judgment on others but there is an expectation that Social Workers will have to protect children who are living in poor, hazardous conditions.

Some homes are very well presented—but always be prepared.

Scenario 3

ALL THE GLITZ AND GLAMOUR

In this case I've been the Social Worker for about two months. Mother has requested that the children come into care. On arrival mother has lost her keys to the door.

My initial point of contact with the mother is to talk through the bay window. Unfortunately this gets us nowhere because the children begin to get upset and confused.

We need to explain our purpose for the visit.

With no other option, I make the decision to climb through the window. Did I mention that I have a knee-length skirt on and the family live on a main road? The kids think it's hilarious to see their Social Worker climbing through the window.

If that isn't enough, we have to take all the children's belongings from the house in and out of the window and then climb back out ourselves.

Definitely a funny image of me I'll always remember.

Tips
Be prepared to do things you did not expect because no day is the same. All my team found it quite entertaining, but, on a serious note, prepare yourself for anything.

Scenario 4

TOO MANY OPINIONS

Meeting with families who already have preconceived expectations for their relative's discharge plans can be difficult, especially if those expectations cannot be met. Such meetings can be made even more difficult when other people get involved.

I visited the hospital ward to see one of my new clients. She had dementia but no previous package of care at home and was at risk of falling due to poor mobility. She was medically fit for discharge with the ward advising that she should go into a placement. However, discharge destinations are not solely the decision of ward staff.

After assessing the lady I went over to the ward desk where there were nurses and occupational therapists. I advised that I would be discharging her to her home with an intensive package of care, usually a maximum of four calls per day and telecare-assisted technology to alert help in the event of an emergency. I was to organise fall detectors and a door sensor so that any evidence of wandering could be identified and help alerted in the event of a fall. I would also be reviewing the case prior to the twenty-eight days usually provided to ensure that the patient is able to settle safely back into her home environment.

After advising the staff nurse of all this and while inputting information into the medical file, I heard a voice say quite rudely: "it would be common sense not to send the lady home". An occupational therapist who was not even working with the patient had decided to add her opinion into the conversation.

Now I am not one to be belittled and I have a full understanding of my professional role. I answered professionally and said: "well it is nothing to do with common sense and the risks identified will be managed and monitored at home".

The occupational therapist then advised me that she had been made aware by her colleague that the lady was at risk of falling and wouldn't be safe at home. I again told her of the support the lady would be provided with upon discharge and we came to a reasonable agreement in respect of the discharge plan.

Tips

There will always be differing opinions with regard to your intervention with it being beneficial to ensure that you have full understanding of the actions you make so that you can be clear when asked.

Be honest from the beginning and let your service users/ families know that intervention in the home is always explored and discussed first.

Your main role is to minimise risks as much as possible which are best assessed within the home, because it is difficult to make a judgment on how someone will manage at home while they are in hospital.

Discharge plans are made based on probabilities and previous information, however if someone has acquired new needs since previously being independent then the first thing is to get them back to their previous level of independence, or at least back into their home environment.

Be clear on what your plan is because this can be challenged by other professionals, by the family and by the service users themselves.

Once you are clear then others will also understand what is happening.

Scenario 5

DAMN REPORTS!

It's 8 pm and I'm still in the office writing reports, which is not unusual in this role. I am practicing as a Senior Practitioner which involves managing complex cases while helping develop newly qualified workers and supporting my fellow peers. I also have my own large case load.

So, why am I entering the eleventh hour of my working day?

I've been having a head to head battle with the Information and Communication Technology (ICT) system for the last hour, nevertheless my reports are finally complete. I have a Child Protection Conference at 10am tomorrow morning, which is what the reports are for.

My brain is no longer working. All week I've been overloaded with writing reports and attending court. I've worked late most nights just to keep on top. On top of everything else, having completed the reports, they now have to be shared with both parents before the conference. Did I mention the conference is at 10 am tomorrow morning? I drive to the parents' house. Yes, I'm undertaking a home visit at 8.45 pm, fuelled by biscuits and cakes because I've not had time to eat. Luckily the visit goes fine with both parents in agreement with the content of the report.

It is now 9:45 pm and I am finally home.

The next morning, I arrive at the meeting and hand my reports over to the admin worker.

I am then told that the reports are on the wrong colour paper and questioned as to whether the reports have been sorted into sibling groups. Now I'm feeling a little patronised. I mean, do I look seventeen rather than my actual age of twenty-seven? This lady is talking to me like I'm a child. I'm growing furious considering all my efforts last night to complete, print copy and share the report with the parents. I want to scream at her but this is also in front of parents and professionals who are waiting for the meeting. I calmly but firmly tell her "the reports are in order, came out of the photocopier at 8.45 pm last night, now let's proceed to the meeting" and this is the politest and most professional way I could have put it.

Tips

Be prepared for working late. Most of the time, no matter how late you work or how much effort you put in, there may always be something you have not done right. The best thing I've learnt is that I cannot do everything perfectly. There will always be barriers: ICT systems, network outages or simply not having the time. Unfortunately, I've witnessed plenty of Social Workers crash and burn out. Do not kill yourself trying. When times are tough and you feel like you are losing sight of what you should be doing, ask yourself these questions: Are the children safe? Are the case records up to date? Have you seen the child? Have you progressed the important, priority matters you needed to progress? And so on. All these questions should be answered with a definitive 'yes' but other questions are less important. Forget if the photocopies are in order and on the right colored paper. Is that your priority in protecting children? Quite bluntly, no. Will this impact on the safety of the children and the implementation of the Child Protection plan? No. Although I respect how different authorities do things, there needs to be some flexibility.

Scenario 6

CALM UNDER PRESSURE

I have a heavy case load: GP respites, imminent discharges, no end of stuff. I receive a call advising, "Help needed in the hospital". 'You have got to be kidding,' my mind whispers. The message tells me to leave all my work, the hospital is on a Level 4 and needs my assistance urgently. Seriously, I'm thinking: "leave my work? Things do not just stop, you know.' But I have to keep that thought to myself.

I arrive at the hospital which is tense with all kinds of manic pressures. Managers' voices come from all ends of the room, saying: "get this assessment done and get discharges quickly; "we need the majority of the patients discharged today into step-down, rehab or home." Now, my main role is working for the step-down team, so if we're discharging people from hospital into the step-down beds and I'm not able to discharge people from the step-down beds because I'm assessing in the hospital, how are the step-down beds going to become free? Common sense could have been utilised but you learn in these situations to leave it to the decision makers because they already have their ideas on what to do. I have to just stay calm, do as many assessments as possible and not let the chaos affect me to ensure that discharges occur that day.

By the next morning I have even more patients added to my list from those that were discharged the night before and emails from the step-down beds requesting urgent discharges due to the pressures now falling on them. I really do thrive on fast-paced work, although it can be very intense working in situations where by resolving one problem you create another.

Tips

Pressure in the hospital can be intense when the hospital is on a Level 4.

You may feel overwhelmed and be called out of your initial role to support other teams irrespective of your current workload and you need to be prepared for this to happen on occasion.

Every day can bring something different in Social Work. Expect the unexpected and try to stay level-headed when everything around you is manic.

Once things settle down, be truthful to your manager about the effect being called away has had on your workload and let your manager know about any extra time required to ensure that those on your workload are not affected by unforeseen circumstances.

Many times you will see a collection of issues arising that you have no control in changing. If you however take the stance to work as a team to facilitate the upper management requests the team will in turn support you in dealing with pressurised situations.

Scenario 7

ASSERT YOUR PROFESSIONAL

Whenever I have disclosed to people that I have worked within a hospital as a Social Worker they ask, "What do Social Workers do in hospitals?"

I'm working with a family who want to look into a nursing placement for their father. A continuing health care checklist has already been filled in, but the service user is not eligible. I have arranged a meeting with the family and ward staff to discuss his discharge plans although I am notified in the morning's multi-disciplinary meeting that the gentleman's needs have become more severe. The multi-disciplinary meetings are meetings held on the ward each morning to discuss progression of discharge. The doctor, ward-sister and discharge-coordinator are usually involved in these meetings. The nurse in charge says, quite rudely, "No meeting needs to be planned" although she never says why.

I have experienced this sort of bluntness many times with healthcare professionals. Some of them do not feel they need to communicate information to Social Workers although you are supposed to be working TOGETHER. Not all nurses are like this of course; I have met some great health care professionals who work well with me and this creates positive results. In this case, I tell the nurse in charge that it is imperative that I am given full information because it is not only required to help me with my next point of contact but to also update the system so as to highlight any changes that are needed. I am then told, by another nurse, that the man is only expected to live a few days. Imagine if I had left the ward without that information and phoned the family to arrange another visit! How inconsiderate and, even more so, how unprofessional would I have looked. Gathering and sharing information is important and I was not going to let the response of one nurse stop me obtaining the information I needed that day.

Tips

Make sure you understand your role and what support you can provide so that you are prepared.

Understand that you are a qualified professional and you have as much right to understand everything that is happening with the patient as any other professionals involved.

Inter-professional practice helps you to provide your support adequately because it gives you an overview of every aspect of the life of the individual for whom you are working.

Do not be deterred by others but state your views and ask questions to support your intervention.

NBSK_BGDSW_int v1-6.indd   21

06/04/2016   09:32:20

Scenario 8

HELPING HAND

"I'm not just here to take away people's children or to tell them negative things, honest," I say.

Mandy screams at me to get out of her house and she does not need to be told how to look after her kids. This is my first meeting with Mandy following a referral from the health visitor who reported poor environmental issues within the home. The referral details that the house is in bad condition. The family has been sleeping on mattresses both on the living room floor and in the hallway.

So far all I have done is knock on the door, been invited in, sat down and asked Mandy how she is. To my shock, Mandy aggressively explodes at me. I do not understand or expect this type of response. She was fine when she invited me in. It takes a while but I calm her down and explain why I'm there. I'm not there to take away her children, I explain.

Mandy and her partner Joe have two children aged eighteen months and a three-year-old and they all live in a one-bedroom flat. Mandy shows me around, by this time she has calmed down after lots of reassurance. The bedroom consists of a double bed, cot and single bed. There isn't enough room to move or "to swing a cat" as Mandy says. The families have no space for bedroom furniture so their clothes are folded and piled high on the beds. Mandy shows me the bathroom; the walls are covered in black mold, as they are in the kitchen. In

22

the living room there are damp patches on the wall covered in mold and there are mushrooms growing behind the sofas. Mandy explains she has been bidding on houses. Bidding is a process whereby applicants wanting council housing are given a number and have to log in online and click 'apply' on houses that will meet their needs. The system then allocates the property to people who have the most need for the property. Mandy has not yet been successful. She becomes tearful and begs me not to take her children away. I repeat that this is not why I am there. She tells me that she's been told—'in the meantime'—to keep the windows open to help with the damp. It's April and still cold. Mandy and Joe have been trying to keep the windows open and are spending an excessive amount on electricity. As a result they do not have the bus fare to go to the library to bid on properties any longer. I can see that this is clearly a housing issue and that the family need support with.

I assure Mandy that I will support her. I complete the Initial Assessment and no concerns are raised about the children.

When I return to the office and speak to the housing department the housing team confirmed the family's situation. I provide a supporting letter which enables the family to be prioritised and placed in a higher band, meaning they will be provided with a suitable property much sooner. It is also agreed that the council will have the mold treated.

Tips

Be prepared for the fact that we are not always wanted in people's homes. Even if our intentions are to support our clients, our title "Social Worker" can be a barrier before we have even spoken.

As Child Protection Social Workers we often get caught up in the statutory tasks that confront us. It is easy to get caught up, but the basics of support go a long way in moving a family forward. It is also important not to forget that when you walk into a situation it is not always what it seems. This family was making the best of what they had and was stuck in a situation they had very little control over. The need to heat the house to remove the mold was making their financial situation worse than it needed to be which, in turn, resulted in them being unable to bid on housing in order to change their situation.

Sometimes families are stuck and it will be your role to support them to bring about change.

Scenario 9

THIS IS WHAT I STARTED SOCIAL WORK FOR:
TO BREAK THE CYCLE

We are in the court room. I am sometimes anxious in court, but this time I feel at ease; I feel proud. Not proud of myself, but proud of Jade, the child's mother who sits next to me. She is very young and grew up in foster care along with her siblings. This is a cycle that some families never break. Jade clearly loves her baby very much. I worked with Jade and her daughter Kasey for five-six months prior to this court hearing.

When I received the case, Kasey was already in foster care, due to significant concerns regarding people Jade was associating with, including her own mother who suffered from significant mental-health needs and was a class-A drug user. Removing a child from its parent is the last resort and is never taken lightly and we always hope that, if possible, children can return to their families. The previous social worker had tried to help Jade to understand the risks and Kasey had been made subject to a Child Protection Plan, but Jade had not been able to protect her baby. Kasey had gone into care under a voluntary agreement, under Section 20 of the Children Act, 1989. The matter was then quickly taken into court and an Interim Care Order was granted.

After Kasey went into foster care, Jade disappeared. She would not speak to the social worker and rarely attended

25

supervised contact sessions with Kasey. The case was assigned to me to continue with the work after the first court hearing.

I had managed to make contact with Jade and had spoken to her in depth regarding what steps she needed to take for Kasey's and her own best interests. I had explained how she needed to change her behavior in order to enable the local authority to consider returning Kasey to her care.

In the court room, Jade shows that she has taken my advice on board and, over the next five months, she engages with everything the Local Authority ask of her. She attends all of the courses available and shows real understanding and learning. Her engagement is fantastic, nothing like I've seen before and all feedback from professionals is very positive. Jade secures herself a place in semi-supported living accommodation in preparation for Kasey to be returned to her.

Following careful consideration by various professionals and an in-depth Social Work assessment the plan is endorsed to return Kasey back to her mother's care, under close monitoring and supervision.

At this hearing, plans are put in place for Kasey child to return to Jade.

The case continues to be monitored. Jade's lifestyle continues to be stable and she is no longer putting herself or Kasey at risk. Most of all, she understands what the risk is and how to keep her daughter safe.

Jade is so excited that the final decision has been made and that her daughter is returning home to her. It is such a lovely feeling to have a good ending. Social workers do love a happy ending.

Tips

Social Work can be an emotional job, especially if you are an emotional person, as I am. There can be many happy endings but, given the nature of the job, they do not happen often. The key to this case was building a relationship with the mother, ensuring she understood what she needed to change and being open and honest with her.

In Social Work, you have to accept that people are in control of their own destinies; parents make decisions, which they alone are responsible for. We weigh their decisions and actions against the risk to the child and the likelihood of this risk continuing. Our job as Social Workers is to give the parents the tools, to try to empower them and to ensure that they know what they need to change.

Of course, in this case, it wasn't all down to me. There was Jade herself and there were other agencies involved. All the skills in the world sometimes can't enable a parent to change; they have to want to change for themselves and have the capacity to change - most importantly, for their child.

Other agencies also build relationships with parents, giving support and helping to enhance parenting skills, knowledge and understanding.

Scenario 10

SUCCESS IN YOUR INTERVENTION

Every Social Worker has a particular case that stays with them.

One particular service user I will never forget was a young, bright and witty teenager who had experienced a lot of trauma in his life leading to frequent episodes of self-harming and to a previous admission under Section 2 of the Mental Health Act.

I remember when I first met him, feeling quite taken aback because I was not much older than him. Straight away, as if he had known me for years, he was able to open up to me and told me that he usually found it difficult to talk with professionals. He felt as if he was generally not listened to because most professionals were too formal in their discussions with him, which in turn made him view them as overly authoritative.

My approach was to communicate with him on his level. One of the things you will quickly learn in Social Work is how to rapidly change your way of communicating, like a chameleon, in order to accommodate yourself to both children and adults. I was able to support him through engagement and, most of all, by listening to what he wanted rather than telling him what he should have. Over time this built trust, the pattern of self-harming reduced and he used to come and talk to me about any frustrations he was

28

experiencing before he self harmed. My intervention was a success although what would happen once my intervention was over I did not know. I left that role and moved to another because it was a temporary contract as a locum worker. Would he keep the skills and maintain the progress we had started? That is always a question I would love to get answered.

Tips
If you ask anyone why they have taken up a career of Social Work, their answer will usually be, 'to help people'. Unfortunately success in your intervention does not always mean long-term success in helping someone. It is important to treat each person as an individual. You may have similar cases, but every situation needs to be looked at as if it is a new situation around that individual's particular needs—because no two people are the same. To achieve success you must use one of the most simple communication skills we first learn as children—to listen. Most people will be more comfortable if they can see that you are really trying to understand their situation—which will, in turn, allow you to intervene and recognise their needs.

Scenario 11

FIRST DAY ANXIETIES

It is my first Social Work placement. It feels strange to have a caseload of real families and real assessments to complete. I am very nervous in case the quality of my assessment is not good enough, although I do not feel alone because this is a general feeling among most students. My first case is a girl aged fourteen. I will call her Sarah. Sarah lives with her granddad. Sarah has been telling everyone in school that she has been having sexual intercourse with males who go to her school. The plan is for me to visit the family together with a more experienced Social Worker while I take the lead, including telling the grandfather about the concerns. That is what I am most worried about! How do I tell a grandfather that his fourteen-year-old granddaughter may be having sex? How do I approach the subject? The assessment visit is at 3.45 pm. All day I am thinking: 'shall I just come out with it and tell him?' or 'shall I dance around the subject?'. I am still puzzled when I get to the doorstep.

Grandfather welcomes us in. He thinks we have come about issues Sarah is having in school. We speak about the school problems for some time. All I can think is, 'how can I tell him about his granddaughter having sex?' The more experienced worker is looking at me. I can see he is urging me to discuss the concerns but they won't come out. I do not feel confident enough. Luckily the more experienced Social

Worker realises I am struggling and he steps in and saves me. He explains to Grandfather that we have had a referral about concerns that Sarah might be having sex. Grandfather is not surprised because Sarah has already told him that the school are worried about this. All of a sudden my anxieties feel very silly. The Social Worker speaks to Grandfather about keeping Sarah safe. I speak to Sarah alone when she denies having intercourse with any boys but says that she did tell people in school she had had sex because everyone else was saying the same. I speak to Sarah about the implications of this and keeping safe and Sarah shows full engagement in the conversation.

So problem solved! I feel I have done well in some aspects. I write up my first Initial Assessment and my manager signs its off with no issues at all... well, apart from a few typing errors.

Tips

Be honest with your manager about things you may struggle with and ask her/him how to approach a subject you feel difficulty in speaking about. Also, speak to other Social Workers in the office and get their advice because they were all new Social Workers once. Remember, even after years of experience there may still be new or tricky situations that you are unsure how to discuss with a family or child.

Scenario 12

WEARING MORE THAN ONE HAT

We are called Social Workers but our role encompasses many different jobs—which can at times be difficult. I mean, I have had to be counsellor, Citizens' Advice Bureau, bearer of bad news, comforter and occupational therapist all in one go. Sounds like a lot right? Well, one situation involved me in having to play six different roles. It was when I was working with a lady whom I will call Emma. Now Emma was around thirty-eight years old and had physical health difficulties preventing her from working which resulted in secondary issues, making her depressed.

I am on a visit because my role is to review Emma's current package of care and to establish what further support can be provided. She is a very articulate and friendly lady. I arrive having used a key safe to gain access, due to her restricted mobility. I then follow her voice into her living room when she says 'hello'. We discuss how she is currently managing and what support she feels she requires.

Emma becomes teary after a while because the conversation leads onto her family. The counsellor role kicks in as I listen, provide empathy and give recommendations for how issues around family dynamics could be resolved. Then Emma discusses her financial constraints. She has gathered up a significant amount of debt because her physical health needs prevent her from accessing leisure activities which results in her being left in the house a lot, which contributes towards her low moods which result in an increased habit of online shopping.

This shift in conversation brings out the Citizens' Advice Bureau/banker role and we shift through the debts and identify payment plans that will enable her to start to tackle the debts.

Lastly we discuss Emma's mobility because this was the main cause that gave birth to her other issues. I am now an occupational therapist. We discuss heights of equipment, aids to support with mobility, possible exercises and other ways to enhance her mobility. I will later refer her to the occupational therapy team for further support because my role is limited to the provision of equipment.

So many different faces in one conversation, although, I think to myself as I leave: 'thank goodness I've been paying attention in the different training I was provided with -knowledge is definitely helpful!'

Tips

Now not all councils ask Social Workers to order equipment, but I would say that the councils that I have worked for that allow Social Workers to manage minor adaptations are definitely better prepared than other councils. There is a vast amount of training on all sorts of topics outside your main role that I would encourage Social Workers to pursue. I have been on various training courses, from trading standards to training on forced marriage. Take the opportunity to increase your knowledge. This will not only enhance your role but will also create confidence in your practice for those you are working with.

33

There are so many titles, roles and shared responsibilities in social care that it can be frustrating for the people you are working with because they have to go through many hurdles to get different answers.

Educating yourself on an array of roles will enhance your skills and minimise time.

NBSK_BGDSW_int v1-6.indd   34   06/04/2016   09:32:20

Scenario 13

JOSH'S STORY

When I worked with Josh he was fifteen. He had been a looked-after child since he was fourteen and he had twin siblings who were adopted. Josh and his siblings had been known to the Local Authority for a number of years, due to their mother's alcohol misuse and neglect. When aged fourteen Josh was physically abused by his mother's partner who was a violent alcoholic. Mother's partner had a history of domestic abuse with various partners but she had chosen not to end the relationship after the assault on Josh.

Josh struggled to deal with the violence he had witnessed and this manifested itself in his own behaviour. There had been a number of incidents where Josh had been violent towards his siblings and had presented aggressively in the foster placement. It was agreed that Josh would move to a foster placement alone where he could receive more personalised support. Unfortunately, Josh has had to leave a number of foster placements due to his behaviour.

Josh's hours at school were reduced to part time and eventually he had to continue his education with an alternative, part time provider. At fifteen he was only attending half the sessions at his education provider; he was spending time with other young people in the local park. He was frequently returned to his foster carers or education provider by the police.

The main part of my role is to work closely to manage Josh's case with the education provider, his previous school, his mother, foster carer and the police in order to keep Josh on track. Josh's foster carer manages to get him onto a fitness course with a peer mentor. This seems to help Josh have a focus.

A few weeks down the line, I have a phone call from the fostering team advising that Josh has been physically abusive to his foster carers, this despite all the efforts that have been made, including a disruption meeting. Josh is not able to return to his foster placement. At age fifteen—nearly sixteen—Josh is placed in a children's home. He does not settle well although he has a good relationship with me and with two of the staff at the home. I spend a long time trying to engage him in positive activities and giving him guidance and support. I visit weekly. He is known to be smoking cannabis and is frequently reported missing. He is arrested for criminal damage, arson and affray. As the offences are at the children's home and he is on bail he is not able to return there—which is quite common. Now my task is to try to find him other accommodation.

Josh struggles to find accommodation due to his arson offence. I visit a young-people's-supported accommodation residency with him, strongly putting his case forward because I am desperate for him to get a place so that he can be in a positive environment. Unfortunately, his conviction for arson is against him. The accommodation cannot accept him. The only accommodation that will is a hostel. Josh's case transfers to the care leaver's team to support him to live independently. I feel overwhelming sadness with regard to Josh's case and how things have ended up.

Josh manages to find a place on a plumbing apprenticeship It is something he is interested in he attends and is doing very well. He forms a positive relationship with a seventeen-year-old girl on the course and they became very close. I often think of Josh and wonder how he is. After a while I learn that he and his girlfriend are having a baby. He is experiencing some mental health difficulties and depression and is still smoking cannabis. The Children's Services are monitoring the family.

The baby girl is born three months premature and is made subject to a Child Protection Plan following a domestic violence incident. Josh and his girlfriend separate and Josh is using alcohol, cannabis and crack cocaine. I am then informed by the baby's Social Worker that at aged eighteen Josh has been sentenced to three years in prison for actual bodily harm against his girlfriend.

Tips

Josh had experienced trauma and abuse within his mother's care which resulted in separation from her. He had also experienced the loss of his siblings. Frequent placement moves and instability added to his experience of loss, creating an inability to form relationships long enough to meet his needs.

The only tips I have are: prevention, early intervention, support and befriending.

There isn't always something we can do but we need to do everything we can to try and support all children—even if we think it is too late.

Scenario 14

EXPECT THE UNEXPECTED

I ring the doorbell, no reply. I do not understand; Nigel is aware that the meeting is scheduled for today. After a further fifteen minutes, one of the neighbours leaves the flat, which gives me the perfect chance to gain access into the communal part of the building. I walk up the stairs and knock on Nigel's door. To my surprise, a very disheveled man answers . It is apparent within those first five seconds that this is not the man I only met four days prior. He is unshaven, poorly dressed and completely disoriented with no depth or emotion behind his eyes. "How can this be?" I think as he lets me in. Only four days ago he was discharged from a mental health institution with no formal diagnosis. He had been brought in voluntarily and then discharged because the psychiatrists found no reason for treatment. When I met him, he was articulate, well-groomed and gave all the right answers. The only reason I am visiting now is for a quick follow-up to ensure everything is in place for when his sister arrives back home. I am actually working on her behalf.

Nigel has been the main carer for her since the passing of his mother over thirty years ago. His sister had been admitted to hospital after a fall. When she was taken to hospital, he took an overdose because he blamed himself for her fall. The guilt and feeling of loneliness resulted in a night of excessive drinking which lead to an overdose of paracetamol. Luckily for Nigel he left the door open and was found by a neighbour who called 999. Due to being a risk to himself, Nigel was sectioned voluntarily for treatment and, during his section, he would visit his sister on the ward, which was when I first met him. He came across very well although I felt that a follow-up was needed to ensure that the home was safe prior to his sister being discharged. Plus, the neighbour who found Nigel after his overdose, informed me that Nigel had a history of alcohol misuse, so I wanted to ensure that support was provided for both parties to maintain safety for Karen when she returned home. Nigel said he would prepare the house and make sure food etc. was ready for when Karen was discharged. I had arranged the discharge for a Tuesday and have gone to meet with Nigel on the Monday to check that all is in place. That's when a different man answers the door and not the Nigel who spoke so well in the hospital.

The house is clean and there is food in the fridge but what had happened to make Nigel relapse so quickly? I call the assertive outreach team because mental health intervention is required. They advise that they will come out to establish what has caused the relapse. Karen's discharge is delayed in the interim although she wants to return home and be with her brother. The assertive outreach Doctor visits Nigel at home, prescribes some medication and recommends further support for Nigel as an outpatient since he has been previously diagnosed with depression.

Karen is discharged back home because she has the capacity to understand the situation although I ensure that on-going support via a package of care is provided, to help and monitor Karen's wellbeing within her home environment.

Tips

No day is the same in Social Work practice. People can give you the appearance that everything is fine or they may just say the things you want to hear, but underneath the façade they may be struggling with their situation. I had decided to double check things at Nigel and Karen's home prior to arranging discharge. This was not strictly necessary because I had already met with Nigel. If I had only taken Nigel's condition as he presented himself during my initial meeting with him, Nigel would have been left without support, with his sister also being discharged into an inappropriate environment.

If you have an inkling that something is not right, even if you are not expecting something drastic it is always best to double check. Double checking can help in ways you did not initially plan for.

Scenario 15

THE SUBORDINATE SOCIAL WORKER

Sometimes in all jobs there are things we are asked to do which feel quite uncomfortable. Each Social Worker is responsible for their own registration. We are responsible for how we act, what we do and for our own professional conduct. Occasionally however, we do not agree with what we are asked to do. In this case I am an unqualified worker, having finished my degree and I am awaiting my Social Work registration to come through in the post. Although this is a formality, I cannot undertake any statutory Social Work tasks, including Child Protection enquiries, until it does.

A colleague has a concern about a case. A young person has taken some indecent images of his girlfriend on his phone. The pictures have been distributed to a number of people at his school. Our manager calls me into her office. She requests that I do a joint visit with the allocated worker to see the images and find out where they were taken because there are concerns that the pictures may have been taken at an adult male's house. After some discussion, it is decided by management that I am the only person available to go, despite the fact that I am not yet qualified. I tried my best to raise my concerns about my lack of experience, but it makes no difference. The manager assures me that he will take full responsibility for everything.

The visit is quickly completed and the photos viewed as requested and they were indeed sexually explicit. Our findings are written up and the information is passed on to the police to deal with the matter.

Months later I receive a phone call from the police. The caller informs me that by looking at the images I may have committed an offence! The police want to interview me and my colleague under caution. All I can think is that my whole career is over before it has even started.

I speak to a solicitor who assures me that, as long as I had a legitimate reason to look at the photos, I have not committed an offence. I endure the police interview under caution and the information is passed to the Crown Prosecution Service for a decision as to whether to proceed. Two weeks later I receive a letter telling me that no further action will be taken because we had a legitimate reason to view the photos and I had been instructed to do so as part of my job.

Tips

As you can imagine, this situation caused extreme distress to all involved. I later learnt that not even an experienced Social Worker should have been allowed to investigate the matter alone. The matter should have been referred to the police and the images viewed by a specialist police officer.

What I have learnt from this has been to trust my instincts and push for what is right. In future, if I were asked to do something that could potentially put my registration at risk, I can politely inform the manager of the reasons why I should not do it. If they do not agree, I can politely suggest that we seek advice from senior management. It is however important, as a good, tactful Social Worker, that instructions are followed from management.

42

Scenario 16

POKER FACE

It is my first week in a community mental health team and it is important for me to get to know the area and institutions that I will be working in. My role is to work with people both as inpatients, meaning those receiving treatment under a section or voluntarily sectioned, and with those receiving support in the community. I decide to accompany one of the more experienced workers on a few visits to different mental health institutions because he has knowledge of these places that no amount of money can buy. I am amazed at where these institutions are located. I have driven past them many times never knowing what these buildings housed. I guess this makes sense really because it would be rather silly to have 'Institution for the Mentally Unstable' in bold letters on the doors; it would be very controversial and raise concerns for people living in the area. We enter a high-risk, male unit which although I do not want to sound contentious I can only describe as a fish bowl because the males are encased behind a glass window. I look at the staff-to-service-user ratio and think there are hardly enough staff to control a situation if it occurs. The separation of the window does not make me feel any less vulnerable to all these men but little old me poses my face like they do not even phase me and like this is not my first time in a place like this.

43

The men stare at me, some with emptiness behind their eyes, some blowing kisses, following me with their eyes and banging on the window, but I have to ignore their behaviour and keep my composure. Many of the institutions I visit, both male and female, have this uneasy atmosphere due to the unpredictability of the residents although, through it all, I keep a level head and I am not, on the outside at least, phased by any behaviours presented.

Tips

It is important to show self-assurance and self-control even when this is not what you are feeling inside. There will be many situations when you feel vulnerable or worried but you must try to keep your composure. I believe this is a very important and a confident appearance can keep a situation from escalating.

Confide in your colleagues—there is nearly always someone nearby with more experience than you, who can teach you the skills you need when dealing with unpredictable situations.

Scenario 17

Job Well Done

It is not all negative. Today I am helping an eighteen-year-old girl prepare for independent life. Let's call this young lady 'Kelly'. Kelly has been in care—she is what we term a 'looked-after child' since she was five and has been in her current foster placement for ten years. She has experienced a lot of neglect from her birth mother because her birth mother was not able to meet her basic care needs. Support was provided on numerous occasions to keep her within her maternal home but Kelly's mother was unable to make the changes she needed to make, to look after her daughter and Kelly came into Local Authority care. Kelly has had contact with her birth mother throughout her life however and they have a good relationship. I have been Kelly's Social Worker for two years. Kelly has a fantastic relationship with her foster carers, but now she feels it is time to live independently.

Separation from home and family can be a traumatic experience. The trauma can impact on a child's development, attachment behaviour, and functioning. This can impact on their ability to function and settle in their foster placements. Lots of children in care move from foster placement to foster placement and this results in them not being able to form the stable relationships they need in order to thrive, grow and

45

develop. Young people in care can find it difficult to move to independent living for a variety of reasons, including lack of parental support while growing up and troubled or unstable backgrounds. The lack of parental and family support can expose them to even greater risks once they are no longer in care. Thankfully Kelly has benefited from a positive experience with the care system. She is very much a part of her foster carers' family and she sees them as family. She will continue to have their support throughout her adult life. Kelly's foster parents keep in contact with a number of children they have fostered and prepared for independent living.

The accommodation is a flat not far from her foster carer and fifteen minutes from the college that Kelly attends. She is studying to be an electrician. Today's task is a nice one. I do not get to do this often, but I'm taking Kelly to a supermarket to buy everything she needs. Her furniture is already in the flat. It was partly furnished and her foster family and the Local Authority have helped with the rest. Kelly is lucky to have been prepared well for independent life, I do not have to do much prompting. She is already familiar with all the kitchen utensils she needs. She picks up everything she needs for her bathroom.

We go back to Kelly's new flat and I help put all her things where they need to be. It is not much, just the basics. I am really happy for her. It just shows—when things work well, the care system can provide children with the stability, care, attention and support they need. What a shame that this is not the same for every child.

46

Tips

There are parts of the job of Social Worker that I do not enjoy but there is a lot that I do enjoy. When things get hard remember the positive moments, reflect on them and remember. There are lots of Kellys. Kelly had a good support network, a fantastic stable placement and the support of her mother. This took years of planning. It is imperative to ensure that all looked-after children have a circle of professionals and loved ones around them to guide and support them. Kelly was a star herself, but around her she had a supportive foster carer, Social Worker, fostering Social Worker, mother, school, college, reviewing officer, health professionals and many more. If we work together as dedicated professionals we can only give a better outcome for all vulnerable children.

Scenario 18

TEAM PLAYER

Duty teams are always busy because you are expected to resolve situations from escalating throughout the day. I arrive one morning to work on the duty desk which I have to do once or twice per week in the team I am working with. You know when you have that feeling that it is going to be a longgggg day? Well, I have got it, and my intuition is correct today—this is going to be a very long day indeed. Phone calls come in fast: from people relapsing to family members concerned about the state of their relative's homes. Then a call comes in and this is a safeguarding call. A concern has been reported by a neighbour that the lady living across from him, whom I will call Kelly, was outside having quite a heated argument with her partner and the argument was looking to appear physical. Kelly is under social services and is allocated to a worker who is on annual leave, hence the call coming through to the duty team. Kelly is eighteen years old with mental health difficulties and receives support due to previous self-harm.

After taking down all the information and quickly briefing my manager for guidance, my first protocol is to try to contact Kelly, but that brings no success. I then call the Vulnerable Police Officers (VPO) because this is obviously a vulnerable situation and I will need support when visiting in case there are physical 'activities' in the home. Let's just say, it is a

48

wasted call; no VPO's will come out with me. I then ask my colleague whether he has any prior engagements and whether he can come out with me. My colleague advises on having a pre-arranged visit which he can put back and we agree to attend to Kelly's house.

We knock on the door, no reply. No one appears to be in. I then proceed to call the office who advises that Kelly returned my call after leaving the office and said she was fine.

Kelly attends her outpatient appointment the next day to pick up her prescription and presents with no issues despite allegations reported by the neighbour the previous day.

Tips

When all else fails, you need to make sure you are a team player and that your colleagues, in return, will assist you when support is needed.

It is never practical or safe to go out on your own when there are associated, highlighted risks.

Being a good team player also helps when you have clients who are untruthful. A witness will cover your back by accompanying you. I have assisted colleagues by just sitting during a visit, as a presence, so that nothing my colleague says can be misconstrued.

Being a team player in Social Work helps with advice, with visits and generally with getting through your job day to day.

Scenario 19

HOW DO I DO THIS?

This week I am in melt down. I have had a case that was stable "blow up", Social Work slang for 'something serious has happened'. This means that 100% of my attention will need to be put onto this case for a long period of time and all other priorities will go out the window. I deal with the case but then I have to go through the task of catching up because I have reports to write, court work to prepare, visits to undertake, supervised contacts to arrange—and no time at all to get it all done in the few hours I have left of the day. I am at breaking point and decide to do something about it. Usually I just get on with it and muddle through, but I feel like I am burning out, so I speak to my manager.

After explaining things to him, my manager delegates some of the tasks that admin can do to an admin worker, gives my note pad to the typist and some other tasks to a Social Work assistant. This helps get some of the small stuff out of the way—and small stuff takes up a lot of time—so I can spend time on the bigger things.

Tips
Never be afraid to ask for help. It is not a sign of weakness; everyone in every profession needs help. Burnout in Social Work is a common problem. There is a high level of sickness

due to stress. If you see a colleague asking for help, help them if you can. It is also important to invest in newly qualified Social Workers because they need lots of help and support in order to become good Social Workers.

Scenario 20

MAINTAINING DIGNITY

As a Social Work student it is a requirement that you complete a certain number of days on placement each year. My last year of placement involved a split between a day centre and a social services care management team. The day centre placement specialised in dementia service users and was attached to a community church.

Each day I would go in and prepare activities that would help stimulate the service users. I remember doing sensory classes and bingo and I actually learnt how to knit from three ladies whom I will call the "knitting crew". Before this placement I would never have imagined myself working with older adults because I had always had my focus set on working with children and families. I was a teenager at the time and it had never crossed my mind to work with this age group—although I truly found the whole experience to be enriching.

My main responsibilities were more to do with the social aspects of care and any personal care tasks were managed by the carers that worked at the centre fulltime. I did not really want to be involved in personal care because, as far as I was concerned, I wasn't a carer and I never believed I should be involved in those sorts of responsibilities in my Social Work practice. How wrong I was!.

It is a normal afternoon. Everyone is settling down after dinner and some of the service users were participating in the exercise activities. The staffing levels are a little low but certainly manageable. Another worker and I are in the main lounge although she is quickly rushed away to attend to a service user who has soiled himself leaving me on my own. I get up to put a board game away in the activity room and, as I am walking past the toilet, which is the next-door room, I hear a voice say, "Help please".

I open the door and standing there is Joan, a frail lady with pearly white hair who is trying to empty her bowels. Joan catches my eye and repeats, 'help me please?' It is pretty clear that she does not know what she is doing because she is wiping herself with her hands and the faeces are getting into her nails. There is no one else to support her. I close the door and ensure she is clean, put a fresh incontinent pad on her and wash her hands. There is no time for me to be finicky because maintaining her dignity and personal hygiene at that moment is paramount.

Tips

I wanted to add this story because, although personal care is not considered to be a Social Work task, it is beneficial in your practice to be prepared to have to help people in different circumstances.

There will be many times when you may visit someone and it is evident that they need some support or prompts with daily living tasks. Do not leave them sitting there but remember that they are people and that their dignity, even if they do not understand things fully, should always be a priority.

I am not one to give support with certain tasks when it is evident that there could be a manual-handling risk involved, so leave those sorts of tasks to the carers when possible. But other things such as making a drink or assisting someone to the toilet—providing they have no unusually demanding problems with their mobility—can and should be undertaken.

Scenario 21

TRUST YOUR INSTINCT

I'm trying to interview a parent for an assessment; it is not going well. Mother, Diane, is very agitated. Diane is from Lithuania and she has four children. She has come into the office requesting financial support. I have to complete a certain assessment to see if we can legally support her since she has no recourse to public funds. This means she is not entitled to any state benefits. Throughout the assessment Diane screams and shouts at me when I try and speak to her. She bangs the table which makes us jump, which is very intimidating to me and my colleague. Diane screams at her children very close up in their faces although they do not flinch at all. They look very neglected. The family are homeless. Diane shows various letters concerning urgent health appointments that she has not attended to for the youngest child.

Twice, I go and speak to my manager and ask that we terminate the interview and seek assistance from the police. I do not feel right about this interview. My manager asks me to complete the assessment. I maintain that nothing is working and I cannot calm Diane down nor get the information I need. I am worried about the children's welfare and Diane's behaviour continues to grow more aggressive and erratic. A number of times I stop the interview and seek management advice. I am told to continue with the interview while the manager speaks to the police. The police arrive, but they do not seem convinced about the urgency of the situation. Higher management have agreed for all four children to stay with a family member and the police will protect them. The police try to speak to Diane but she grabs her handbag and takes out a hammer. She is waving it around and screaming and shouting. The police intervene and I manage to get the children out of the way to a secure place. Diane is sectioned under the Mental Health Act because she has a number of bottles of pills in her bag which she could take to induce an overdose. She is discharged with support from the mental health team. The children remained with family members.

Tips

While at work it is important to be aware of your own safety. Always have someone with you if you are unsure about a situation. If you are going out of the office, sign in and out with the address of where you are heading. Alert someone if you are visiting a family you have never visited before. It is important to read the history of a family and identify if there are any violence markers highlighted on the address in the file.

When undertaking a home or office visit, sit closest to the exit door. If delivering difficult news to a family, decide where the best place might be to deliver it e.g. at the office? or at a police station? Think about the nature of the concerns and whether you need to be supported by another colleague in case of false allegations.

Also, trust your instincts. Know when to stop the conversation and how to read people's behaviour. Being able to deflate situations and calm people down is a skill that will help—although issues may arise that are beyond such calming behaviour, perhaps when dealing with mental health difficulties or drug or alcohol abuse.

Scenario 22

NO FAMILY OR FRIENDS

We all aspire to get a good job, buy a nice house and live independently for as long as possible until decisions on our welfare need to be made by our next of kin.

Well, I learnt very quickly, through working in various older-adult teams, that not everyone has someone to support them with important decisions later on in life.

There was one gentleman whose circumstances stayed with me as I had tried endlessly to adhere to his wishes.

I will call this gentleman, John. Now John had lived his life independently for many years in a beautiful, old Victorian house which had been his family home from birth. He was admitted to hospital following a fall. I am sure he would never have believed that the day he left his home in the ambulance would be the last day he would see his home.

I supported John in a rehabilitation unit aiming to get him back to his previous level of function but then he had to be re-admitted to hospital due to further deterioration in his overall health following his initial fall. After physical intervention in hospital he was asked his thoughts about his discharge plan. He was severely hard of hearing but he had the capacity to understand written communication.

I remember asking John on three occasions what support he would like to be provided with upon discharge. John was aware that his need for support had grown and that he now

58

needed support with his daily living tasks. He asked to be discharged home with a package of care. The only issue remaining was John's home environment—the ambulance that had taken him to hospital in the first place had recorded that John's home was uninhabitable without a deep clean.

I requested, with John's consent, that he be transferred to a step-down bed as an interim measure while further assessing his home. I remember driving up this lavish road with beautiful big houses on either side. John's house stuck out like a sore thumb; the garden was overgrown and the front appeared tired compared to the other houses on the road. I opened the door and was immediately hit with a strong smell of faeces—he had been keeping stray dogs and they had used his front room as their own personal lavatory. His home gave witness to a history of self-neglect although he was not previously known to social services.

I organised for a few cleaning companies to accompany me on a visit so as to provide quotes which I would later share with John because he would have to fund the clean independently. Following this I went over the quotes with him although he had acquired a lack of engagement and he also advised that he did not have access to any money. In previous, similar situations I have been helped by family and close friends to gain information on finances etc. Unfortunately John had no one: no family, no friends and no next of kin. I remembered seeing his admission report which had also reported dehydration and malnutrition. Things started to make sense. John could not access his money nor pay for food to look after himself. For weeks on end I tried to support him by accessing some funds available through the department although his health continued to deteriorate.

59

A discharge home would no longer be safe or appropriate and John himself agreed to twenty-four-hour care.

I felt so bad that his initial wish to return home could not be made possible although I collected things from his home to make his room in the care home more comfortable. But by the time the payments and finances were finally set up he had passed away.

His home still remained and I remember the care home manager asking who should receive his belongings left in the care home—and thinking to myself, 'no one'.

Tips

I have had colleagues who have attended funerals when people have passed away with no close friends or families.

Not everyone has family support and such people, I feel, require a little extra care to facilitate their needs.

Display empathy and understanding. I used to visit John to have little discussions with him not simply to ask him about his finances but for further social interaction. The care home he ended up in was also fantastic and integrated him into their activities.

Although I wanted to support John to return home, in the end he passed away in a caring environment, with people around him rather than on his own. He had made the decision to stay there independently.

Scenario 23

DADDY MADE ME HIT MY HEAD

In this instance I am a student Social Worker out with a more experienced Social Worker. A five-year-old child, "Bobby", is in his head teacher's office. All he has said is, 'Daddy hit my head'. Bobby has a large bruise and cut on his head. This is what we call a Child Protection matter, because Bobby has said he is injured and that an adult caused the injury. Local Authorities have a duty to investigate. The police have spoken to the Social Work managers (this is called a 'strategy discussion'—where police and Social Workers decide how to investigate the matter). It is decided that an experienced Social Worker will go out first and speak to Bobby to find out what has happened. This case seems quite interesting to me at this point because I have only been on my placement for two weeks. I decide to shadow the Social Worker and we arrive together at the school. Mother is in reception very distressed and upset. The first thing she says is, "you're not taking my child away". This is a line I have heard many of times in my Social Work career.

We reassure mother and enter the head teacher's office. I have not been in a head teacher's office since school and I feel like a school kid again. The Social Worker sits mother down and asks if she knows about the bruise. After lots of tears and shouting mother states that she was out at the time the injury happened. Following this, the Social Worker

61

speaks to Bobby alone, which is normal procedure. Bobby states that his father grabbed him and hit his head on the table because he was being naughty. I am thinking, 'gosh this sounds serious'.

Bobby's sibling, Katie, who is seven, is also spoken to alone. Katie is asked to tell us about how Bobby hurt his head, and she says that they were both running round the house and their dad had told them to stop running but they did not listen. Katie says that Bobby went to run through the living room and dad tried to catch him and Bobby fell and banged his head on the table. Katie is asked if Bobby was upset, she says, he was and that there was lots of blood all over the place but it was an accident.

Father is spoken to separately from the children and gives exactly the same account as Katie. Bobby is spoken to again and confirms that he was running through the living room being naughty and that he hit his head.

According to the accounts given separately by Katie and by the father, Bobby hit his head accidentally. Due to Bobby's age he was not fully able to explain how the injury occurred and his account made things seem a lot worse than they were in reality.

Tips

Referrals are not always what they seem on paper. The most important tip is to always speak to the child and gather all the information. The voice of the child is the most important part of what is happening within a family unit. Over the years I have developed various methods of communicating with children of different ages and abilities.

It is important to be able to enable children to open up to you quickly. This may mean using different communication tools such as drawing, colouring books, dolls to play with and toy cars, or it may be a simple as to start a conversation about spider man or one direction to enable children to feel comfortable to express themselves.

It is also important that only Child Protection-trained professionals speak to children about Child Protection concerns. Any practitioners whom children make disclosures to should immediately report those disclosures to children services and only ask the child where, when, how and who—minimal questions but producing enough information to make sense of a referral. It is important not to ask leading questions or put new words into the child's mouth.

Scenario 24

VIRUS SEASON

Swine flu! Norovirus! C-diff! That's all you hear in hospital during the winter months, everyone waiting to hear what the next virus will be.

There was one year in particular that I got caught up in all the fuss. I started to feel a bit sick and not my usual self. It was only my second week within a new role in the hospital and how could I be sick already? I mean, I washed my hands regularly and used antibacterial gel although I still did not feel good. I worked the whole day although I really did not feel right. That night I felt terrible—I experienced vomiting and diarrhea to be exact. It felt like my insides wanted to change places with the outsides. Okay, maybe a bit too much information, but, believe me, it was the worst sickness I had ever encountered.

I did not know what I had caught but thought it might possibly be norovirus. Next day I could not even move, let alone go into work. Two days off and then a weekend was what it took for me to fully recover.

And all because I went to assess in areas where the virus was known to have struck. Never ever again.

Tips
I have worked in many environments where there has been a range of contagious illnesses from scabies to gastric infections.

It is crucial that you have an understanding of the environment in which you will be working in order to ensure that you can protect yourself correctly.

Social environments such as schools, residential homes and hospitals spread infections more freely. Occupational health experts can support you with any concerns you may have regarding your own health and concerning any lack of immunity, this is especially important when pregnant.

There are always protocols to be followed and in some environments your role as a Social Worker will not be required until the infection is clear.

Managers may expect you to work in conditions where known there are viruses but hold your ground and do what is healthy for you. Remember you cannot work if you are sick, and you will be more valuable well and can catch up on unfinished cases or paperwork when you return.

Scenario 25

THE DARK SIDE OF SUMMER, CHRISTMAS AND FOOTBALL

Most jobs have their busy times. Gardeners have more work to do in the summer and less in the winter and plumbers the opposite. Believe it or not, in Child Protection we also have our busy times. I did not really notice this until I worked in a team dealing with all of incoming referrals regarding concerns over children.

In the summer holidays you would think it would be quiet, on the assumption that most of our referrals come from schools but this is not the case. We have a massive peak before the six-week holidays, usually from schools wanting support for families who may struggle over the six weeks' break. We also get more referrals regarding children being left home alone due to parents struggling with work commitments or due to general neglect of their child's needs.

Then there's Christmas. A happy time?—not for all families. Due to high consumption of alcohol during the festive season, disputes over Christmas contact, family-and-couple disputes and disputes due to financial pressures, there is a high level of domestic abuse over the Christmas period. During the World Cup domestic abuse also rises, leading to more calls to the police and more referrals from them to Childrens Services. **One police force in England and Wales calculates** that violent incidents increase by 38% when

66

England lose but also rise by 26% when they win, Each domestic abuse case where a child lives in the household and the police are called will be screened by Childrens Services and the police jointly. Some cases will require intervention from Childrens Services. This intervention may involve support services, counselling, preventative work or a social-work assessment to see if the child is at risk of harm

There are huge peaks in referrals when children return to school following a break such as the six-week summer holidays. When they return back to school this is often when children disclose incidents that have happened during the holiday. Since this usually happens within the first week or two of returning back to school, this can be a very busy period.

These peaks in referrals can have a major impact on Social Work teams if local authorities do not have the capacity to deal with a surge. Referal numbers cannot always be predicted.

Tips
Of course we cannot predict and plan for every event for every child. However, at a case by case level, as a Social Worker it is imperative that you in-tune to social and family events that may impact on the families you work with.

Potential risks to the children you work with long-term may change depending on external factors.

When we can predict a change in behaviour or a change in clients' ability to cope, we should risk-assess this and change support plans for the family where possible.

Scenario 26

Do You Have Kids?

I walk into the room and set up my chair over by the table, making sure that I have a good enough position to observe but that my presence will not be involved in the interaction between parent and children during this supervised contact session.

It is definitely a little difficult because the room arranged for the contact session is rather small. The foster carer brings the children in and then leaves. About ten minutes later mum comes in.

Both kids run to her and mum greets them with sweets and donuts and their eyes light up. Then, as the kids munch their way through the goodies, mum gets a glance at me. I usually wear a pair of jeans and a jumper to supervise contact because it can be best to be less formal—with children especially. When you are observing interactions between families, smart clothes can make them feel less comfortable.

Following her glance, mum decides to address me, saying: "you look young to be doing this job. Are you old enough?" In the back of my mind I want to say, 'Really? Do you think someone under eighteen can do this job?' But the ever-professional person that I am just says, "yes I'm old enough" and then, to put the focus back on the children, I ask Sarah, the youngest child, to show mum her picture that she has been drawing while waiting. I say this to prevent discussion of my age from turning into a conversation. Mum then decides it is question time. "So, do you have any children?" she asks. I say: 'no I do not—but this is your supervised contact with your children". Then she says, in quite a harsh tone: "how would you know about what should be happening with these children when you do not have any?". She seems more interested in me than what she is there for. I change the conversation once again, to interaction of the kids which I think made her get the point that this was not up for discussion. I mean, really, if I had said what I really wanted to say like: 'I do not have to have children to understand the reasons why contact has been established in this way in your case.' But no I just smile, stay professional and keep my attention on supervising the contact. At the end of the day that is the Purpose of my involvement.

Tips

Never become offended by people or react in a way that is unprofessional. They will have their own thoughts about you based on how you look but it is your role to keep the focus on what is at hand. It is not appropriate to discuss your life with the service users you are working with.

Silly comments will come from both service users and other professionals. So many times, other professionals have said foolish things—and I say foolish because they should know better. I have had to get used to: "wow you only look about sixteen" and "you do not look old enough to be doing this job".

Now obviously I have to be over twenty-one to be a qualified Social Worker. The best way to reply to such comments is to show people that you do your job professionally. Showing your capabilities despite other people's perceptions is always a winner I feel.

Scenario 27

WHAT WE REALLY DO

Some think Social Workers sit in houses drinking tea and chatting; others think we are the modern-day equivalent of the child catcher in Chitty Chitty Bang Bang; others that we are there to serve them as adults. The truth is far from such people's perceptions. Here is a typical day:

I walk into the office; its 9.15 am. Today my diary is empty. This does not mean I will do nothing; it means that I shall write four reports for a Child Protection conference and update my case records from all my interventions over the past few days. However, as soon as I step into the office, the duty worker, Chloe, who takes calls and deals with emergencies if the allocated worker is not present, approaches me. Chloe informs me that she has received a call from the police about a domestic violence case already allocated to a Social Worker. The mother of the children was hit over her head by the father and sustained a head injury. The parents have been separated for three months following an incident in which father was intoxicated and a heated verbal altercation took place which resulted in him being arrested. Since the incident, the two children have been subject to a Child Protection Plan with an agreement in place for mother not to have any contact with father. Father has recently arrived at the house and assaulted mother breaking his bail conditions.

I assist Chloe in speaking with mother at the hospital in respect of arrangements for the children and mother's immediate plans. After a lengthy discussion, mother decides to go into a women's refuge to ensure that she is safe. This will enable mother to have daily support and monitoring and gives a better chance of mother being supported in maintaining her separation from father. Chloe makes a phone call to acquire about a place in a women's refuge for mother and the children. Meanwhile there are no family members or friends who can care for the children over night. With both parents' agreement, the children are placed in an emergency foster care under a voluntary Section 20 agreement while mother recovers in hospital. The following day mother and children are taken to a women's refuge. None of this involved drinking tea or snatching children.

Tips

Often in this job, things do not go as planned. Social Work is a complex job involving law, policies and lots of hands-on practical work. It is important that, as a Social Worker, you can adapt to any situation and be flexible no matter how demanding or serious the issue may be.

The social-work ethos is for children to remain with their parents where possible although, of course, the welfare of the child is paramount.

Where possible we try to support families to live together and, if it is safe to do so, arrangements can be made to keep families together during a perod of crisis. In this case it was the role of the local authority to provide the very short-term care and make safe arrangement for the mother and her

72

children, while all along considering on-going risk assessment of the situation and considering all options available to the children. No situation can be risk free when children remain at home, especially those on a Child Protection Plan. It's about reviewing and managing the risks as a multi-agency group and taking action to safeguard children if the risks become unmanageable.

In this case it was important to look at support for mother to leave the relationship with father and enable her to take steps to protect her children. This is not always possible and it does not always work.

Scenario 28

LOCUM SOCIAL WORKER

They do not teach you during your degree about the benefits of becoming an agency Social Worker. Well, I have been an agency Social Worker since I first qualified and I would not have changed my journey for anything. You can gain a wide array of experience because you are in control of your contracts; you can spend a year in one place, gain the relevant experience and then move onto to another while increasing your pay.

I started in care management for adults, then moved over to hospital Social Work, then community mental health teams and learning disabilities teams for children while constantly increasing my rate of pay as I became more experienced. Okay, so money is not the main reason I moved from one type of work to another and, to be honest, I would stay in a position for at least a year to ensure a level of consistency for the service users I was working for, but the experience is brilliant for enhancing your knowledge at turbo speed compared to a more permanent position. My initial move, when embarking on the world of the locum, agency worker, was to register with an agency—which was the easiest task of all because agencies want you on their books. I remember being bombarded with emails because I had signed onto four agencies advertising Social Work jobs everywhere. I later realised that they all pretty much advertised the same jobs and I quickly decreased the number I was registered with. This helped me because it reduced a double-up of referrals sent by the agencies which must have been an annoyance for all concerned.

Although the money and experience are great, every job has its negatives including locum Social Work. People's expectation can be difficult to manage—when starting a locum job you do not have the probation period provided when you start a permanent job. Your role is to work efficiently at a good pace adding to the level of support already provided by the team you are to be involved with. Starting my new position in the transitions team caused me some anxiety because it involved a mixture of both adult and children's Social Work practice. I walked into the office on my first day and was expected to start taking cases and organising visits while, at the same time, learning the process from other colleagues. Thank goodness for those colleagues!. They really enabled me to get through that job.

Computer systems can also be a bit of a headache. One would think that with all these local councils so close to each other they would use similar systems. Do they just! That would be too easy, I guess.

There are pros and cons to being an agency worker but, all in all, it works for me.

Tips

You can become a locum Social Worker either when newly qualified or later on in your profession. It may not work for everyone because you must learn to adapt—since different jobs have different processes. It is always good, however, to

75

see what jobs are available, in particular if you are trying to gain more experience.

You also need to take into account your need for the benefits that come from being employed permanently, such as sick pay if you have health needs, or, simply, you need to take into account what is right for your family and you as a practitioner.

Scenario 29

IS THIS WHERE IT ENDS?

I feel blessed to have been involved in so many different parts of people lives. I've held the hand of a child who trusted in me and told them "It will be ok", I've supported families through the loss of their child while we investigate what's happened to them. I've worked with families at their most vulnerable but also at their strongest. Although this has been challenging I truly feel proud to be part of such a hard-working, dedicated profession.

On the other side, this is a job that sometimes takes everything you have out of you. Sometimes you feel physical symptoms from the stress working in Child Protection. The night when you can't sleep or when you do finally get to sleep you wake up in the middle of the night worrying about what you have and have not done or what you need to do. Sometimes the job is impossible. It's like juggling fifty balls at the same time and you can't drop one. Everyone wants something and everyone's something is urgent. It doesn't matter if you're working till midnight sometimes it's impossible to do everything that they expect of you. Statistics are very important. I might have written three court reports and four Child Protection conference reports and placed a child in care. There are no weekly statistics for that work. However there is data produced in regards to have I visited children on time, have I seen the child alone, have I had core group meetings and is there a chronology on the file. This may seem sensible, but if you have a few weeks where you have to prioritise court work and still manage to do the things that are statistically recorded but physically have no time to enter it on to the ICT system it looks like you have not done the work. So you will still be chased as if you have not done the basics, when infact your working above and beyond.

Every area of Social Work brings a different type of stress and different priorities.

It sounds like I do not like the job, but the truth is I do, I love it. I love the fact that my skills, relationships and how I work with other people have safeguarded so many children.

I love being part of an organisation that changes children's lives—even though the system is far from perfect and I do not think it ever will be.

I admire people who remain in Social Work for thirty years, I really do not know how they do it. It takes a very special person; I'm not sure if I'm that person. Where do I go from here? I do not know.

Tips

Seek support from management and colleagues, always speak about how you are feeling. This job can't be done in isolation; the emotions and the seriousness of the day to day issues are things we can't deal with alone.

A good manager will listen to your stresses and offer support. There is only one you, so do not burn yourself out.

Scenario 30

A LIFE CHANGING CAREER

Each day I awake to help someone. Whether big or small the purpose of each day is to provide some sort of positive outcome into a child, adult or a families life.

An even if the goal I set out achieve to help someone does not occur that day, at least I know that is why I came into this profession.

To have the opportunity to learn about people from all walks of life.

To learn about different cultures, traditions, mental health, physical health conditions, communications skills, family dynamics,advocacy,analytical skills,interpersonal skills, resilience and legislation that governs practice,

Okay I could go on an on an on... But they all have helped develop my own responses in my personal life.

And after all the skills taught, to then put them into practice to help someone smile and see light in a period of darkness far outweighs the stresses that arise.

So through it all the ups and the downs i must say social work has been a life changing profession for me.

79

Glossary

Care Plan: A document that outlines a child's needs and how the Local Authority will meet them while in Local Authority Care.

Continuing Care Assessment: NHS 'continuing healthcare' means a package of on-going care that is arranged and funded solely by the NHS when an individual has been found to have a 'primary health need'. Such care is provided to an individual aged eighteen or over to meet needs that have arisen as a result of disability, accident or illness.

Chronology: A document that outlines the main events in a family's life in date order

Care Proceedings: Care proceedings are usually held in the Family Court and more complex cases may be held in the, County Court or High Court. Care proceedings can be brought by the Local Authority under Section 31 of the Children Act 1989 if there is concern that the child concerned is suffering or is likely to suffer significant not harm and that it is in the best interests of the child to intervene.

Core group meeting: Statutory 6 weekly meeting involving multi agency professionals and the family that shares information, review the progress of a child protection plan and the risk to the child.

NBSK_BGDSW_int v1-6.indd   80   06/04/2016   09:32:21

Child Protection Conference: A chaired multi-agency meeting which decides if a child is judged to be suffering, or is likely to suffer, significant harm and therefore needs a Child Protection plan in place to reduce the risk.

Child Protection Plan: A plan put into place for a child who is deemed to be suffering or likely to suffer significant harm while. The plan will contain short-term aims and long-term actions for parents, Social Worker and other agencies in order to reduce the risk and to further assess the risk to the child.

Assertive Outreach Team: Assertive outreach teams (AOTs) are specialist mental health teams. Referrals are made from the community mental health team for people who present with severe mental illness find it difficult to work with community mental health teams (CMHTs). Referrals can also be made for complex needs such as: violent behavior, serious self-harming, not responding to treatment, drug or alcohol use and mental illness (dual diagnosis), unstable accommodation or are homeless.

Crown Prosecution Service: The principle public prosecuting agency for conducting criminal prosecutions in England and Wales. Its main responsibilities are to provide legal advice to the police and other investigative agencies during the course of criminal investigations, to decide whether a suspect should face criminal charges following investigation and conduct prosecutions both in the magistrates' court and crown court.

Domestic Abuse: Abuse within a relationship this maybe between partners, or family involving physical, emotional, economic or emotional abuse

81

Discharge Plan: Each hospital will have its own policy and arrangements for discharging patients. Normally, when you arrive in hospital, the professionals in charge of your care will develop a plan for your treatment, including your discharge or transfer. This is usually done within twenty-four hours of your arrival.

Minimal Discharge: Most people who are discharged from hospital need only a small amount of care after they leave. This is called 'minimal discharge'.

Complex Discharge: If you need more specialised care after you leave hospital, your discharge or transfer procedure is referred to as a 'complex discharge'. For example, you may: have ongoing health and social care needs, need community care services, need intermediate care be discharged to a residential home or care home.

Eid: An important religious holiday celebrated by Muslims worldwide that marks the end of Ramadan, the Islamic holy month of fasting.

Intermediate Care: Intermediate care is a concept within the wider category of health care. Alternative support is provided outside of hospital for rehabilitation, for further assessment or to prevent bed blocking. Funding is provided by both health and social care services within an environment where the patient's needs can continue to be managed after transfer from hospital and prior to their final discharge destination. Intermediate care teams consist of: occupational therapists, Social Workers, physiotherapists, nurses and rehab. staff.

82

Interim Care Order: An Interim care order is granted by the court for eight weeks if it feel a child has been at risk of significant harm or the child is likely to suffer significant harm and it is in the child's best interest to make an order. An Interim Care Order allows the local authority to share parental responsibility, to place the child in Local Authority care or with a family member. The order is usually renewed by the court by consent of parties while the care proceedings continue, until a final decision is made.

Key Safe: A key safe is a strong mechanical metal box that securely stores a key for access to your home. It is installed into brick or concrete on the outside of the property and your keys are accessed by a combination code. The combination code is only known to you and those authorised to have access your home.

Locum: Working on a short-term-contract basis, paid on an hourly rate, but no entitlement to benefits such as to sick pay.

Looked-After Children's Review: A meeting chaired by an independent person to review the arrangements, needs and care plan for a child who is in Local Authority Care.

Multi-Disciplinary Practice: Multi-disciplinary teams consist of staff from several different professional backgrounds who have different areas of expertise in both health and social care. These teams are able to respond to clients who have multiple needs requiring the help of more than one kind of professional.

No Recourse to Public Funds: This refers to destitute people from abroad who have no entitlement to welfare benefits, to Home Office support for asylum seekers nor to public housing. Local authorities have a duty to advise people on their personal circumstances and to assist them in finding a solution to their destitution. In limited circumstances, councils can provide care services including accommodation and financial support if certain eligibility criteria are met.

Section 2 of the Mental Health Act: Allows for someone to be compulsorily 'sectioned' for assessment and then necessary treatment because they are either a risk to themselves or to others.

Section 20 Accommodation: A duty placed upon the Local Authority to provide accommodation for a child in their area who needs shelter because either: no one has parental responsibility for them, or they are lost or abandoned, or the person caring for them can no longer care for them.

Supervised Contact: Supervised contact takes place when a child has been removed from a parent when it has been determined by a professional that a child has suffered or is at risk of suffering harm. The parent and child still have the right to maintain contact with each other. Therefore, contact between the child and parent is supervised

Section or Voluntarily Sectioned: The Mental Health Act is the law that defines when you can be admitted, detained and treated in hospital against your wishes, also known as being 'sectioned'. The decision is usually made by three people:

nearest relative, approved mental health professional and specialist Doctor. An assessment will take place and possible treatment will be provided. You can only be sectioned if you are putting your own safety or someone else's at risk.

NBSK_BGDSW_int v1-6.indd   85   06/04/2016   09:32:21

Index

NBSK_BGDSW_int v1-6.indd   86
06/04/2016   09:32:21

Insight

The truth behind Social Work is a realistic down to earth view on day to day Social Work practice and the daily dilemmas faced. Many books were invaluable during our studies and practice, however we wanted to write a realistic view on Social Work, with a light hearted approach.

Our book provides insight into the profession, how variable each day can be and the challenges that arise. We wanted to also provide Tips for Social Workers already in the profession, newly qualified Social Workers and students, to enable them to be prepared for any situation.

This book allows the reader to get into our minds allowing them to find humor, sorrow and joy in our experiences. We wanted to strip Social Work bare and expose the ups and downs of Social Work in the current climate, including our own practice.